Understanding the Elements of the Periodic Table™

NITROGEN

Heather Hasan

rosen
central™

The Rosen Publishing Group, Inc., New York

For my son, Samuel. You fill my heart with joy.

Published in 2005 by The Rosen Publishing Group, Inc.
29 East 21st Street, New York, NY 10010

First Edition

Library of Congress Cataloging-in-Publication Data

Hasan, Heather.
Nitrogen / by Heather Hasan.
    p. cm.—(Understanding the elements of the periodic table)
Summary: Explains the characteristics of nitrogen, where it is found, how it is used by humans, and its relationship to other elements found in the periodic table.
Includes bibliographical references and index.
ISBN 1-4042-0158-0 (lib. binding.)
1. Nitrogen—(Juvenile literature.) [1. Nitrogen. 2. Periodic law—Tables.]
I. Title. II. Series.
QD181.N1H37 2004
546'.711—dc22

                                                      2003022263

On the cover: Nitrogen's square on the periodic table of elements. Inset: Model of nitrogen's subatomic structure.

Manufactured in the United States of America

Contents

Introduction

Alfred Nobel was an engineer and inventor who is best known for his 1867 invention of dynamite. As a young man, Nobel became very interested in a nitrogen-based explosive called nitroglycerin. Nitroglycerin is a liquid that is made by mixing glycerin (an oily, syrupy liquid) with nitric and sulfuric acids. Nitroglycerin is so dangerous that just a small amount can set off a massive explosion. At the time, it was thought that nitroglycerin was too dangerous for any useful purpose. That did not stop Nobel. He believed that nitroglycerin could be very useful as an explosive for blasting rock and for mining.

Nobel and his younger brother, Emil, began experimenting with nitroglycerin in 1859. Over the years, they experienced several nitroglycerin explosions. Then, a large explosion in 1864 killed Emil and several other people. Following the tragedy of his brother's death, Nobel set out to find a safer way to work with this dangerous explosive. Two years later, Nobel himself was nearly killed. While working with a test tube full of nitroglycerin (enough to blow up his entire laboratory), the tube suddenly slipped out of his hand! Amazingly, the tube landed in a box filled with sawdust. The nitroglycerin spilled from the test tube and was absorbed by the sawdust. Not wanting to be wasteful, Nobel used the mixture for his testing. He found that the nitroglycerin was much easier to work with when it was not a liquid. This gave him an idea that would forever change the world.

Nobel began mixing nitroglycerin with other substances. Eventually, he mixed the explosive with a substance called silica, making a paste. This paste could be shaped into rods that would be safe to handle. Alfred Nobel had invented dynamite!

Nobel intended dynamite to be used to make the mining industry safer and more efficient. But his discovery, along with some of his other 354 inventions, became weapons of war. Perhaps out of a sense of guilt or out of a desire to promote peace, Alfred Nobel invented the Nobel prizes. He wanted the money he had made from his inventions to be used for good, to make the world a safer and more peaceful place. Nobel left instructions that,

Chemist Alfred Nobel is best remembered for his work with nitroglycerin, a nitrogen-based explosive. Some of his work would lead to terrible killing devices used in warfare. Later in life, Nobel strove for world peace. The Nobel prizes are named in his honor.

following his death, the fortune he had amassed from his inventions was to be used to reward people for achievements in chemistry, literature, peace, physics, and medicine.

For better or worse, Alfred Nobel's work with this nitrogen-based substance would forever change the world. Nitrogen not only gave the spark to nitroglycerin, but, as you will learn, it is an element we cannot live without. Every day we breathe and eat nitrogen. Simply put, nitrogen is one of the most abundant and important elements on the periodic table of elements.

5

Chapter One
The Origins of Nitrogen

Nitrogen (N) is all around you, but you wouldn't know it. You cannot see it, feel it, or even smell it. In fact, pure nitrogen does not do very much at all. For this reason, nitrogen was originally named *azote*, which is Greek for "without life." However, this name is quite ironic when you consider some of nitrogen's other qualities. Without nitrogen, we would not be able to survive. Nitrogen is found in food, fertilizers, medicines, and our bodies. Nitrogen is also used in dyes and household cleaners.

But don't let nitrogen fool you. There is also a darker side to this element. By combining with oxygen, nitrogen forms pollutants that can harm our breathing. Nitrogen is also used to make violent explosives, which can cause destruction and death. Like many other elements in the periodic table, nitrogen can be harmful or helpful, depending on how it is used.

The Discovery of Nitrogen

Since pure nitrogen gas does not do very much, it took a long time for people to notice it. Nitrogen was not discovered until the late eighteenth century. At that time, scientists knew that air was made up of at least two gases, and many scientists were working hard to determine what these gases were. Though several scientists were on the road to discovering

Nitrogen is found everywhere, from the stars in the sky to the soil to everyday products we use at home. Nitrogen even makes up most of the air we breathe. But while nitrogen is important to life, it can also be used as a main ingredient in destructive forces such as dynamite. Depending on how it's used, nitrogen can support life or destroy it.

nitrogen around the same time, credit for its discovery was given to a Scottish physicist named Daniel Rutherford. In 1772, Rutherford announced his discovery of what he called "noxious air." He named it this because animals could not breathe in it nor could candles burn in a container filled with it.

However, it was not until 1775 that a French scientist named Antoine-Laurent Lavoisier suggested that this "noxious air" was actually an element. It was also Lavoisier who later suggested the name *azote*, which is what the French still call nitrogen today. The term nitrogen was first used by Jean Antoine Chaptal in 1790. This name was created from the Greek words *nitron* and *senes*, which together mean "niter forming." Niter is the common name for potassium nitrate, a naturally occurring salt that was a known source of nitrogen at the time.

What's in Air?

In the late 1700s, scientists did not yet know of all of the gases that are found in the air we breathe. Today, we know the breakdown is this:

Nitrogen (N_2): 78 percent
Oxygen (O): 21 percent
Argon (Ar): 0.9 percent
Carbon dioxide (CO_2): 0.03 percent
Hydrogen (H), helium (He), krypton (Kr), neon (Ne), xenon (Xe), radon (Rn), and other elements and particles: 0.06 percent

Now you know more than Daniel Rutherford and the other scientists of the eighteenth century did!

Nitrogen and the Periodic Table

All of the materials and objects around you are made up of elements or different combinations of elements. There are more than 100 known elements today. Wanting to organize these elements somehow, scientists arranged them on a big chart, called the periodic table. The periodic table that we use today is based on the work of a Russian chemist named Dmitry Mendeleyev. Mendeleyev published the first version of the table in 1869. He came up with the idea of the periodic table while teaching chemistry at the University of St. Petersburg in Russia. Mendeleyev sought to organize the elements in a way that would make it easier for his students to study and understand them. He arranged the elements in horizontal rows, according to weight, with the lightest element of each row on the left end and the heaviest one on the right.

Nitrogen is identified by the letter N on the periodic table. The number 7 in the upper-left corner represents the element's atomic number. This is the number of protons contained in the atom's nucleus. The number 14 in the upper-right corner identifies the element's atomic weight. This is the sum of protons and neutrons in the atom's nucleus.

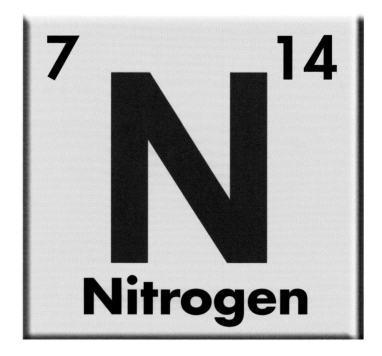

Though Mendeleyev's periodic table did not list all of the elements that we know of today, nitrogen was among those that he included on his first chart.

Uut and Uup Get on the Table

When Mendeleyev designed the periodic table, he left gaps to allow room for newly discovered elements. Over the years, more than fifty new elements have been added to the table. In fact, new elements are still appearing today. In January 2004, two new elements were created by a team of Russian and American scientists. Element 113 is named ununtrium (Uut); element 115 is named ununpentium (Uup). Because of these elements' enormous atomic weights, they are known as super-heavy elements. However, the existence of ununtrium and ununpentium have to be verified by other scientists before they are given a permanent place on the periodic table.

Chapter Two
The Element Nitrogen

Each element is made up of only one kind of atom and cannot be broken down into smaller parts. This means that every atom of nitrogen is exactly the same. Atoms are also very tiny. It would take 200 million of them, lying side by side, to form a line only 0.4 inches (1 centimeter) long! In order to fully understand what makes the nitrogen atom unique, we have to look at things that are even smaller than atoms—subatomic particles.

Subatomic Particles

The three main subatomic particles that make up an atom are neutrons, protons, and electrons. Neutrons and protons are clustered together at the center of the atom to form a dense core called the nucleus. Neutrons carry no electric charge, while protons have a positive electrical charge. This gives the nucleus an overall positive electrical charge. Nitrogen has seven protons in its nucleus, so its nucleus has a charge of +7.

Around the nucleus of an atom are negatively charged electrons, arranged in layers, or shells, around the nucleus. The electrons are not fixed in a single position but orbit, or circle, the nucleus. The negative electrons are attracted to the positive nucleus, and it is this attraction

Nitrogen Snapshot

Chemical Symbol:	N
Discovered By:	Daniel Rutherford in 1772
Classification:	Nonmetal
Properties:	Nonreactive, nonflammable, colorless, odorless
Atomic Number:	7
Atomic Weight:	14.00674
Protons:	7
Electrons:	7
Neutrons:	7
Density at 293 K:	0.0012506 g/cm^3 at 1 atm
Freezing/ Melting Point:	-345.82°F; -209.9°C; 63.25 K
Boiling Point:	-320.44°F; -195.8°C; 77.35 K
Commonly Found:	Air, soil, stars

that holds the electrons around the nucleus. The electrons are not pulled all the way into the nucleus because the negatively charged electrons repel each other. The number of protons and electrons is equal, so the positive and negative charges of the atom balance. Therefore, since nitrogen has seven protons, it also has seven electrons.

All Elements Are Unique

What makes nitrogen different from other elements such as oxygen or silver (Ag)? The difference lies in the number of protons that are found in the nuclei of their atoms. Since it is the number of protons that makes each element unique, it makes sense that the elements on the periodic table are organized by these numbers.

The number of protons that are found in the atom of an element is called the atomic number. On the periodic table, this number is found above and to the left of an element's symbol. Since an atom of nitrogen has seven protons, its atomic number is 7. The fact that nitrogen has seven protons in its

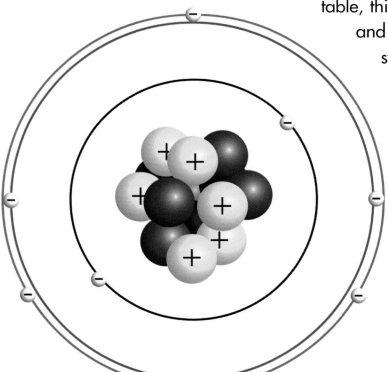

An atom of nitrogen contains seven protons and seven neutrons in its nucleus. Seven electrons orbit, or circle, the nucleus. The nitrogen atom has two shells of electrons.

nucleus is what makes it nitrogen. Let's imagine that we could add a proton to nitrogen's nucleus (which is actually physically impossible). Now its nucleus would no longer have seven protons; it would have eight. We would now have an atom of oxygen. We cannot breathe without oxygen. Just one proton makes the difference between an element that allows us to breathe and one that doesn't. If we were able to take away one of nitrogen's protons, we would have carbon (C), which has six protons in its nucleus. Carbon is very different from nitrogen. While nitrogen is a colorless gas, we see carbon in the form of diamonds and coal or the graphite in your pencil. As you can see, changing one little proton can make a world of difference!

Atomic Weight

The number that is found above and to the right of an element's symbol on the periodic table is called the atomic weight (also called atomic mass). The approximate atomic weight is the sum of the number of protons and neutrons in the atom. Nitrogen has an atomic weight of 14. When we know the atomic weight of an element, it helps us to figure out how many neutrons there are in an atom of that element. Knowing that the atomic weight of nitrogen is 14 and the atomic number (number of protons) is 7, we can figure out how many neutrons there are in an atom of nitrogen by subtracting the two numbers:

$$\text{Atomic Weight} - \text{Atomic Number} = \text{Number of Neutrons}$$
$$14 - 7 = 7$$

As you can see, nitrogen has seven neutrons in its nucleus. We can find out a lot of information about nitrogen just by looking at the periodic table!

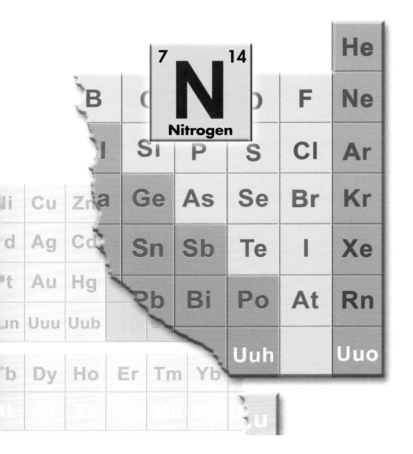

Nitrogen is located to the right of the periodic table's staircase line. This placement puts nitrogen with the other nonmetals on the table. At room temperature, nitrogen is found as a gas. However, nitrogen can be cooled to become a liquid. This process takes extremely cold temperatures (–320.44°F; –195.8°C). Nitrogen is located in group VA, also known as the nitrogen family. This group includes nitrogen, phosphorus (P), arsenic (As), antimony (Sb), and bismuth (Bi). In this group, nitrogen is the only element that naturally appears as a gas.

Arranging the Periodic Table

Unlike Mendeleyev's chart, the elements on the periodic table that we use today are listed in order of increasing atomic number (number of protons). Arranged like this, many trends, or patterns, can be seen. You can use these trends to help you classify the elements. By locating where an element is found on the periodic table, you can predict whether it is a metal, a nonmetal, or a metalloid, which is a substance with characteristics of both a metal and a nonmetal.

If you look at the periodic table, you will notice that the elements are divided by a "staircase" line. The metals are found to the left of this line, and the nonmetals to the right. Most of the elements bordering the line are metalloids, or semimetals. These act like metals sometimes and other times like nonmetals.

Nitrogen is found to the right of the staircase line. This is where you would expect to find it, since nitrogen is a gas. A nonmetal is an element that does not have the characteristics of a metal. Metals are shiny, flexible, malleable (they can be pounded into sheets), and ductile (they can be pulled into wires). They are also good conductors of electricity and heat. By contrast, nonmetals are not shiny. They also do not conduct heat or electricity well. Nearly half of the nonmetals are colorless gases, but they can also be liquids and solids. However, unlike solid metals, solid nonmetals are brittle and will crumble or break apart if pulled upon or hammered.

Many times, nonmetals are found combined with other elements. Some nonmetals, however, are very important to us in their elemental, or uncombined, form. Nitrogen is one of them. When nitrogen is not combined with other elements, it is always found as a diatomic molecule.

Diatomic Molecules

The word "diatomic" means "two atoms." A diatomic nitrogen molecule contains two nitrogen atoms and is written N_2. There are only seven elements, including nitrogen, that form diatomic molecules like this. The other six are hydrogen (H_2), oxygen (O_2), fluorine (F_2), chlorine (Cl_2), bromine (Br_2), and iodine (I_2). If you look at the periodic table, you can see that these diatomic molecules (excluding hydrogen) form the number seven. This is a good way for you to remember these special elements.

Groups and Periods

The periodic table is very useful for many other reasons. An element's location on the table will tell you a lot about the element. As you look

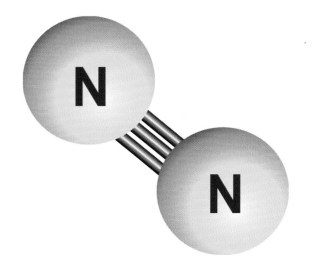

Two nitrogen atoms bond to create the diatomic nitrogen (N_2) molecule. It is formed by strong triple bonds. Diatomic nitrogen is the most abundant gas in the earth's atmosphere.

across the table from left to right, the horizontal row of elements is called a period. Elements are arranged in periods by the number of electron shells that surround the nucleus of their atoms. Nitrogen is in period 2. Therefore, the electrons in a nitrogen atom occupy two shells around its nucleus.

As you read down the chart from top to bottom, the column of elements you see is called a group or family. Just as you might have similar characteristics to the other members of your family, the elements in a given group have similar properties. Nitrogen heads the family of elements that make up group VA.

The Nitrogen Family

There are five elements in group VA, or the nitrogen family. They are nitrogen, phosphorus, arsenic, antimony, and bismuth. Looking down group VA from top to bottom, you can see that the elements become more metallic. That is, the elements begin to take on more and more

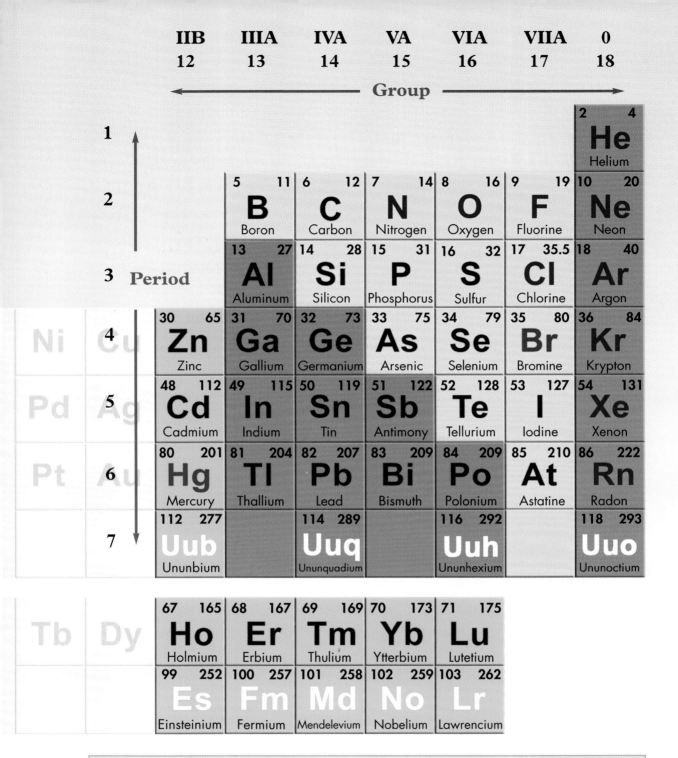

On the periodic table of elements, nitrogen is found in group VA and period 2. As you read down the table, from nitrogen to bismuth, the elements in the nitrogen group become more metallic. Arsenic is located along the staircase line, which separates metals from nonmetals on the periodic table. Elements such as silicon (Si), arsenic, and tellurium (Te) are metalloids, meaning they have properties of both metals and nonmetals.

properties of metals. Nitrogen and phosphorus are nonmetals, arsenic and antimony are metalloids, and bismuth is a metal.

Nitrogen has two shells of electrons surrounding its nucleus. The inner shell contains two electrons, and the outer shell has five. All of the elements in group VA have five electrons in their outermost shell. These outermost electrons are called valence electrons, and they determine how an element acts. Because they all have the same number of electrons in their outermost electron shell, all of the group VA elements have similar chemical properties. The chemical properties of an element are the properties that involve chemical change.

All elements have characteristic properties. These properties help scientists identify them. There are two types of properties, chemical and physical. The physical properties of an element can be observed without changing the identity of the element. Some examples of physical properties are color, freezing point, and phase at room temperature. Chemical properties can be observed by how an element changes its identity after a chemical reaction. Chemical properties include the way an element bonds or reacts with other elements, such as in the chemical reaction of combustion.

Gaseous Nitrogen

At room temperature, an element is found in one of three physical states: solid, liquid, or gas. Knowing the physical state, or phase, of an element at room temperature helps scientists to identify it. Nitrogen differs from the rest of the elements in its family because, at room temperature, nitrogen is a gas.

Gases, such as nitrogen, do not have definite shapes or volumes. If put in a container, a gas will take the shape of the container. Gases differ from solids and liquids because they are able to be compressed and are able to expand. Gases will fit in a container of almost any

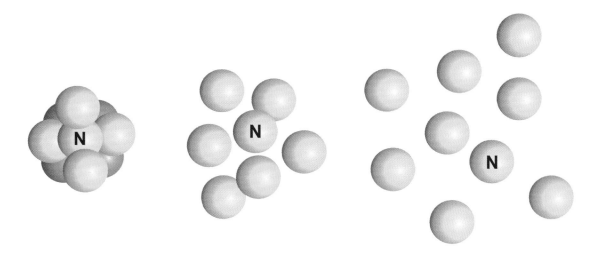

Like atoms of other elements, nitrogen atoms have different densities at different phases: solid, liquid, or gas. As a solid *(left)*, the nitrogen atoms are clustered closely together. As a gas *(right)*, the nitrogen atoms are more spread apart. Changes in temperature can cause nitrogen to change phases.

shape and size. If put in a large container, a gas will expand to fill it. It can also be compressed to fit into a smaller container. If not confined to a container, gases will disperse into space.

Cooling Nitrogen

Naturally, nitrogen is always a gas. However, if this gas is cooled to a low enough temperature, nitrogen can become a liquid or even a solid. In order for nitrogen to condense, or turn into a liquid, the temperature must be -320.44°F (-195.8°C). That's cold! As a liquid, nitrogen is colorless and odorless, resembling ordinary water.

For nitrogen to reach its freezing point (the temperature at which it becomes a solid), the temperature has to drop even further to -345.82°F (-209.9°C). Not even in the coldest places on Earth do the temperatures drop that low! In fact, the coldest temperature ever recorded on Earth is -129°F (-89°C), nowhere near nitrogen's freezing point.

Density of Nitrogen

Density measures how compact an object is, that is, how much mass it contains per unit volume. Solids are denser than liquids, which are, in turn, denser than gases. Solid nitrogen has a density of 1.03 g/cm^3. This is just a little higher than the density of liquid nitrogen, which is 0.81 g/cm^3. In comparison, the density of water is 1 g/cm^3. Gaseous nitrogen has a much lower density than both solid and liquid nitrogen. Its density is only 0.00125 g/cm^3. These densities can give you an idea about how far apart the nitrogen atoms are in each of these phases. The atoms in solid nitrogen are packed very closely together. The atoms in liquid nitrogen are not as closely packed, but, as with solid nitrogen, they still touch one another. However, the nitrogen atoms in gaseous nitrogen are quite far from one another. In fact, these atoms are so spread out that the volume of the gas is on average about 750 times greater than that of a sample of solid or liquid nitrogen of the same mass.

Diatomic Nitrogen

When two nitrogen atoms meet, they lock together very tightly to form a diatomic molecule. In the diatomic nitrogen molecule, both atoms share three pairs of electrons with the other atom. When two atoms share electrons in this way, the link they form is called a covalent bond. In covalent bonds, the atoms share either one pair (two electrons), two pairs (four electrons), or three pairs (six electrons). The more electrons the two atoms share, the stronger the bond is. Nitrogen atoms share three pairs of electrons. This is called a triple covalent bond.

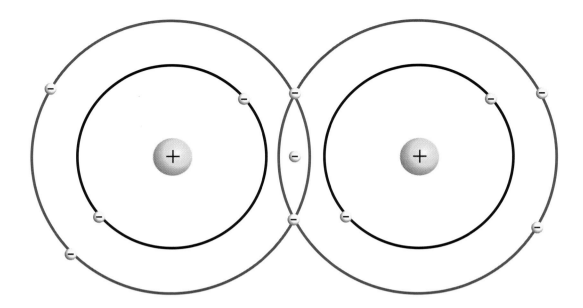

Diatomic nitrogen is formed by a strong covalent triple bond between two nitrogen atoms. This triple bond is the sharing of six electrons between the two atoms. A massive amount of energy, such as that found in lightning, is needed to break apart the strong covalent bond.

Triple bonds are very strong. The triple bond between the atoms in the N_2 molecule makes it very stable and unreactive. Because the nitrogen atoms are so tightly bonded to each other, they do not normally react, or combine, with other substances. Scientists call nitrogen and other unreactive substances like it "inert." In order for nitrogen to react with other elements, the strong bond between the nitrogen atoms must first be broken. This takes a lot of energy!

Chapter Four
Where Can Nitrogen Be Found?

Nitrogen is one of the most abundant substances in the universe. It is found in the stars, in the Sun, and in meteorites. Nitrogen is also found in Earth's atmosphere. In fact, nitrogen gas makes up 78 percent of Earth's air. That is about four times greater than the amount of oxygen found there. In fact, every breath you take is mainly nitrogen. Because the atmosphere contains so much nitrogen, it is a neverending source of the element for commercial use.

Getting Nitrogen from the Air

There is a lot of nitrogen in the air, but before it can be used, it must first be separated from all the other gases that are found in air. Most commonly, nitrogen is obtained from air in a process called cryogenic distillation. In this process, air is cooled until it becomes a liquid. Air liquefies at about -274°F (-170°C) and between 8 and 10 units of atmospheric pressure, where it becomes a boiling liquid. Each of the elements in the air turns back into a gas as that particular element's boiling point is reached. Scientists know that nitrogen has a boiling point of -320.44°F (-195.8°C). At that temperature, nitrogen leaves the liquid air as a gas. Since none of the other elements in the liquid share nitrogen's boiling point, nitrogen can be separated from the other elements.

Liquid nitrogen begins to boil when exposed to air. The steam around the jar *(above)* is condensed water vapor from the air, which forms from the extremely cold temperature of the liquid nitrogen. Liquid nitrogen is commonly used in the food industry to freeze products. It is also used in medical procedures.

Scientists wait until the temperature of the liquid gas reaches -320.44°F (-195.8°C), and they collect the nitrogen gas as it comes out. Once the pure nitrogen has been isolated from the mixture, it is ready to be used commercially, either in a gas or liquid form.

Nitrogen and the Food Industry

Liquid nitrogen is used often in the food industry. Liquid nitrogen is so cold that it allows foods to instantly reach temperatures far below freezing. Freezing things at such low temperatures is called cryogenic freezing. Foods like fruit and cheesecake are packaged and then sprayed with

Liquid nitrogen freezes food so quickly that the food cannot lose moisture. Losing moisture is one of the main causes of food spoilage. Liquid nitrogen can also be used to preserve a food's flavor. Prior to the use of liquid nitrogen in the food industry, many consumers complained that food products lost their taste after being artificially frozen.

liquid nitrogen. Upon contact, the liquid absorbs the heat from the food and evaporates, leaving the food frozen. The food is then ready to be shipped or stored. Foods treated with liquid nitrogen freeze so quickly that the food does not have time to lose moisture or grow bacteria, as do foods that are frozen by a normal process. Because foods that are frozen by liquid nitrogen are not significantly damaged as they freeze, they turn out fresher and better tasting when thawed.

Gaseous nitrogen is also used in the packaging of food. That "air" inside your potato chip bag is not air at all. It is nitrogen. Here, nitrogen does more than just keep your chips from getting crushed. It also keeps them from going stale. If the bags were filled with regular air, the oxygen in the air would react with the fat in the chips and make them stale. Nitrogen does not react with the chips, so they stay fresh. They stay fresh, however, only until you open the bag. Once you open your bag of chips, the nitrogen gas escapes and is replaced by air. Then it is only a matter of time until your chips lose their crunch.

Nitrogen and Health Care

Food is not the only thing that can be frozen by liquid nitrogen. The rapid freezing of liquid nitrogen can also be used in the health care

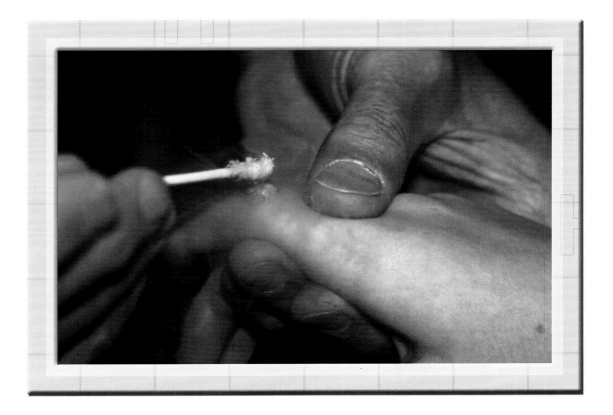

Liquid nitrogen is also very useful in the health care industry. Here, liquid nitrogen is applied to a wart. The liquid nitrogen is so cold that it kills the unwanted skin tissue. This treatment is called cryosurgery.

field to preserve important materials. The liquid can be used to freeze blood so it can be stored until it is needed. Liquid nitrogen can also be used to freeze viruses that will be used for vaccinations at later dates. Gaseous nitrogen, because it is not reactive, can also be used to package some medicines. The nitrogen keeps the medicines from absorbing moisture or reacting with oxygen, two things that can greatly reduce a medicine's effectiveness.

Nitrogen can also be used by surgeons. Skin and other human tissue will die if it is exposed to very cold temperatures. This is usually called frostbite. Surgeons take the basic idea of frostbite, but with the use of liquid nitrogen, they are able to kill unwanted or unhealthy tissue on the human body by controlling which body tissues come into contact with the cold temperatures. Liquid nitrogen provides the extreme cold needed to remove warts, tattoos, birthmarks, and skin cancers. Surgeons treat the infected area with a small amount of liquid nitrogen or use a super-chilled scalpel to scrape away the unwanted tissue.

Chapter Five
Nitrogen Compounds

Elements chemically combine to form compounds. For nitrogen to combine with other elements, the nitrogen (N_2) molecule must first be broken apart. Breaking the strong triple bond that holds the nitrogen molecule together takes a lot of energy. Most organisms are not able to supply the kind of energy it takes to break a triple bond. However, even though they do not have the ability to use nitrogen molecules directly, plants and animals are full of nitrogen compounds. How is that possible? In order to get the nitrogen they need to grow and survive, plants and animals must rely upon what is called nitrogen fixation. Nitrogen fixation is the high-energy process of converting nitrogen molecules into the nitrogen-containing compounds that plants and animals can use. Most nitrogen is fixed in one of three ways: atmospheric fixation, biological fixation, or industrial fixation.

Atmospheric Fixation and Nitrogen Oxides

One way to break a nitrogen molecule's bond is to expose it to heat. Heat is a form of energy. When a molecule is exposed to heat, the atoms get excited and move very rapidly. If enough heat is added to a molecule, the atoms will move so much that the bond holding them together will break. The stronger the bond, the more heat, or energy, it takes to break it. Since a nitrogen molecule (N_2) has a very strong triple bond, it takes extremely high temperatures to separate the atoms.

Lightning provides the kind of heat that is needed to break nitrogen bonds. When lightning flashes, it can heat the air as high as 60,000°F (33,000°C)! After the nitrogen molecule splits in two, the nitrogen atoms are free to react with oxygen. When nitrogen and oxygen combine, they form a compound called nitrogen monoxide (NO). Nitrogen monoxide is a colorless gas that is made up of one nitrogen atom and one oxygen atom. Nitrogen monoxide then reacts with other oxygen atoms

Lightning affects nitrogen during atmospheric fixation. The massive heat released by the lightning breaks apart the bonds of diatomic nitrogen in the atmosphere. The separated nitrogen atoms then bond with oxygen atoms to form nitrogen monoxide. This eventually leads to other compounds that enter the soil and help trees and plants grow.

in the air to form a compound called nitrogen dioxide (NO_2). This compound is made up of one nitrogen atom attached to two oxygen atoms. Nitrogen dioxide is a poisonous reddish brown gas with a very pungent odor.

Reactions in the air and soil convert these nitrogen oxides into soluble nitrogen compounds that can be easily absorbed by the roots of plants. Once the nitrogen is inside a plant, the plant uses it to make more complex nitrogen compounds, such as chlorophyll. Nitrogen is one of

Nitric acid (HNO$_3$) reacts with the element copper (Cu). A penny (which contains copper) is placed in a beaker and nitric acid is added *(left)*. The reaction causes a brownish gas and blue-green liquid foam to be released *(center)*. The reaction then releases nitrogen dioxide *(right)*. Nitrogen dioxide is the same harmful substance that forms following atmospheric fixation.

the elements found in chlorophyll, and plants need chlorophyll in order to undergo photosynthesis. That is how plants make their food. Without fixation, the nitrogen that plants need would not be available to them.

Biological Fixation and Ammonia

Biological fixation is the process by which most nitrogen compounds are made. In this process, bacteria in the soil convert nitrogen gas into ammonia (NH$_3$). Ammonia is a compound made up of one nitrogen atom and three hydrogen atoms.

Nitrogen-fixing bacteria are the only living organisms that are capable of using nitrogen directly from the air. Instead of using heat to break the nitrogen bonds, however, these bacteria use an enzyme. An enzyme is a molecule that speeds up a chemical reaction. You can

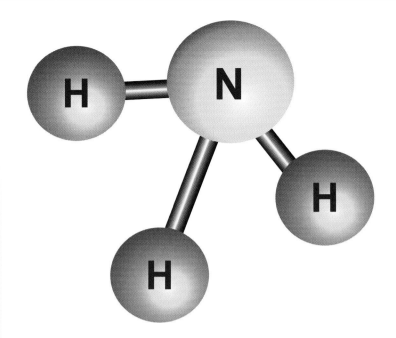

In biological fixation, bacteria use an enzyme to break apart the strong bonds in diatomic nitrogen. A freed nitrogen atom can then bond with three hydrogen atoms to form an ammonia molecule. Ammonia is a key ingredient in fertilizers, which help plants grow.

recognize an enzyme because its name usually ends in "-ase." The enzyme that bacteria use to convert nitrogen into ammonia is called nitrogenase. Once the nitrogen bonds are broken by this enzyme, the enzyme helps the nitrogen bond with three atoms of hydrogen, forming ammonia (NH_3). Ammonia in the soil can then easily be converted by other bacteria into compounds that plants are able to absorb. This way, certain plants can get the nitrogen they need.

Industrial Fixation

The useful nitrogen compound ammonia can also be made synthetically in a process called the Haber-Bosch process. This process, like atmospheric fixation, uses very high temperatures to break the triple bonds. However, instead of using lightning as a heat source, the Haber-Bosch process uses natural gas. Atmospheric nitrogen gas is combined with hydrogen gas (H_2) at temperatures of about 932°F (500°C) and pressures of about 300 atmospheres. Metal catalysts, which work in a similar way to the enzymes used in biological fixation, help to speed up the reaction.

Despite the large amount of nitrogen gas in the air, it is often a lack of usable nitrogen in the soil that keeps plants from flourishing. This problem of not having enough nitrogen in the soil can be solved by the ammonia that is produced in the Haber-Bosch process. Ammonia from the Haber-Bosch process can easily be liquefied or combined with other elements and used as a fertilizer for plants. Ammonia is a vital ingredient in fertilizers, and you will see just how important it is when you look at the nitrogen cycle.

The Nitrogen Cycle

The nitrogen cycle describes how nitrogen and nitrogen-containing compounds change as they move throughout nature. From the air, nitrogen passes to the soil, to all living things, and then eventually back into the air. We have already discussed how plants get their nitrogen from the soil through nitrogen fixation, but what about animals? Unlike plants, animals cannot make their own food. Animals must get their nitrogen by eating plants, which have absorbed nitrogen from the soil. Animals also get nitrogen by eating other animals, which have fed on plants. The nitrogen that is locked in the tissues of these plants and animals is released during digestion. Animals are then able to use nitrogen to form complex nitrogen-containing compounds, such as protein, in their bodies.

The cycle continues when plants and animals die. As dead plants and animals decompose, or break apart, they deposit complex nitrogen compounds into the ground. Certain bacteria that live in the soil break

The nitrogen cycle begins with atmospheric nitrogen. Bacteria in the soil absorb nitrogen and turn it into ammonia. Additional bacteria turn the ammonia into nitrate, a nutrient. Plants then absorb the ammonia and nitrate. Animals then eat the plants, thus consuming the nitrogen as a nitrate. When the animal dies and decomposes, the nitrogen is released and reenters the soil or the air.

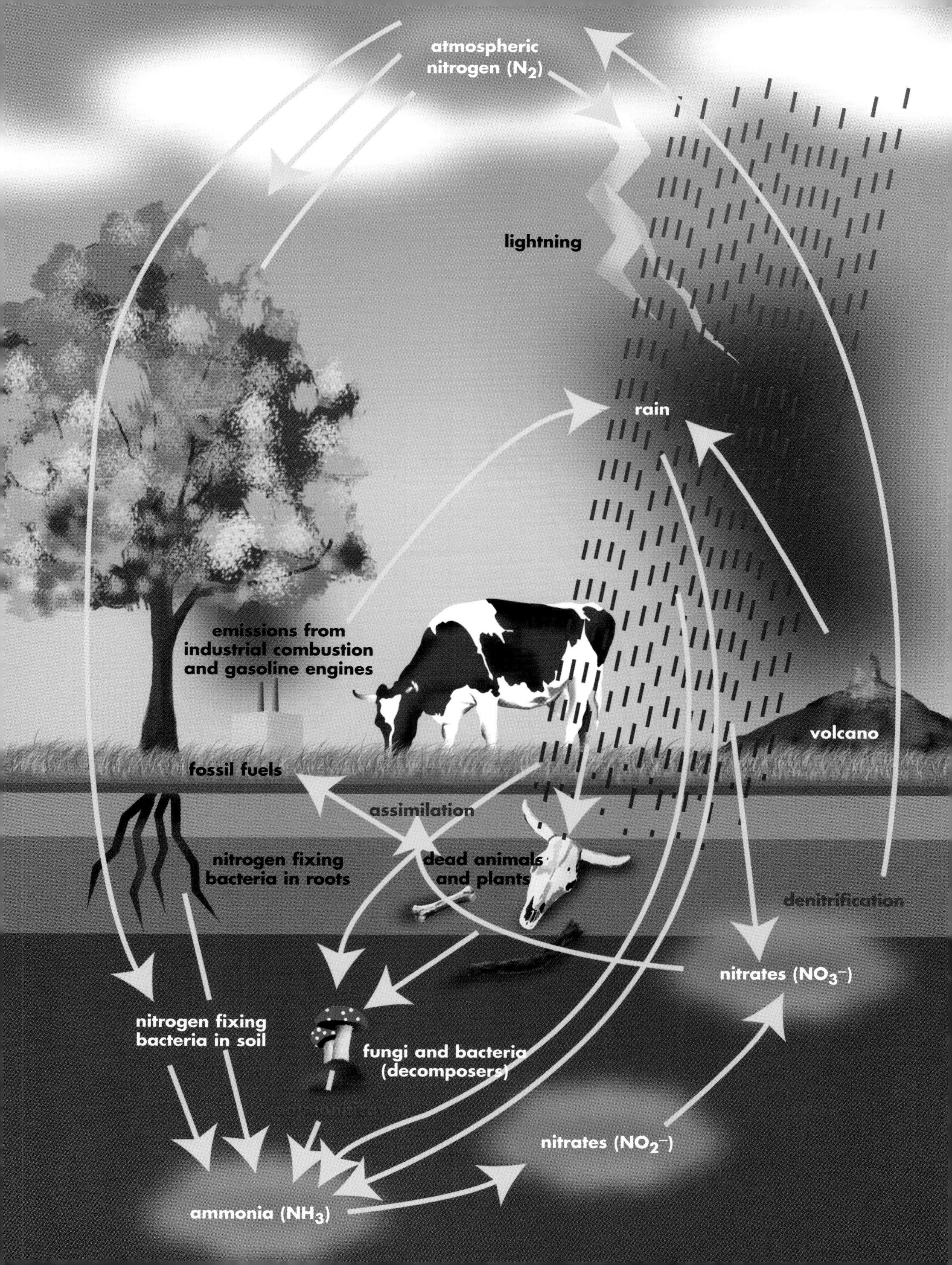

atmospheric
nitrogen (N₂)

lightning

rain

emissions from
industrial combustion
and gasoline engines

fossil fuels

assimilation

nitrogen fixing
bacteria in roots

dead animals
and plants

volcano

denitrification

nitrogen fixing
bacteria in soil

fungi and bacteria
(decomposers)

nitrates (NO₃⁻)

nitrates (NO₂⁻)

ammonia (NH₃)

down these nitrogen compounds, turning them back into ammonia. Some of this ammonia is converted by bacteria into soluble nitrogen compounds, which can be reabsorbed by plants. Other bacteria work to turn this ammonia back into nitrogen gas, which is returned to the atmosphere. Because plants and animals are dying and decomposing all the time, the nitrogen cycle stays in balance. Nearly the same amount of nitrogen gas is returned to the air by these bacteria as was taken out by other bacteria. This completes the cycle and keeps the nitrogen content of Earth in a perfect balance.

Nitrogen Compounds in Your Body

You now know how your body gets nitrogen, but what does it do with it? Your body uses nitrogen compounds to make important nitrogen-containing molecules such as protein and DNA (deoxyribonucleic acid). These molecules are so important that you would not be able to live without them.

Protein is found throughout your body. It gives your body its structure, organizing your tissues and organs and giving them strength

Nitric acid (HNO_3), which contains nitrogen, can be used to test for the presence of proteins. Milk, which contains many proteins, can be used to demonstrate this test. After a small amount of nitric acid is added to a jar of milk *(left)*, the acid reacts with the proteins, turning the milk a yellow color. The yellow color comes from the rings on the amino acids (building blocks of proteins) being infiltrated with nitrogen from the nitric acid.

Dangerous Nitrogen Compounds

Although Alfred Nobel appreciated the usefulness of nitrogen compounds, he also knew firsthand how dangerous they could be. One of the main uses of nitrogen is the making of explosives. One of the first explosives ever used was gunpowder, or potassium nitrate (KNO_3). This compound was invented more than 1,000 years ago. Today, two nitrogen compounds that are commonly used in explosives are trinitrotoluene (also called TNT) and nitroglycerin. TNT is the explosive that is used in bombs, and nitroglycerin, as you know, is the explosive part of dynamite.

Why are these nitrogen compounds so explosive? It is because they are extremely unstable. They are unstable because the nitrogen atoms in them are eager to re-form diatomic nitrogen molecules (N_2). Diatomic nitrogen molecules, with their strong triple bonds, are, by contrast, very stable. Remember all of that energy that had to be added to the nitrogen molecules to get them to form compounds? That same amount of energy is released when the compound breaks apart and nitrogen gas is able to re-form. The nitrogen gas expands very quickly. It is this incredibly fast expansion of gas that is the actual explosion. A tiny spark, a flame, or heat is all that is needed to get an explosion started. Some nitrogen explosives, such as nitroglycerin, are so sensitive that they will explode when simply shaken or moved.

and flexibility. Protein is in your hair, your skin, and your muscles. Without it, you would not be able to run down the street or even to take a breath. (Your lungs and other organs are made with protein, too.)

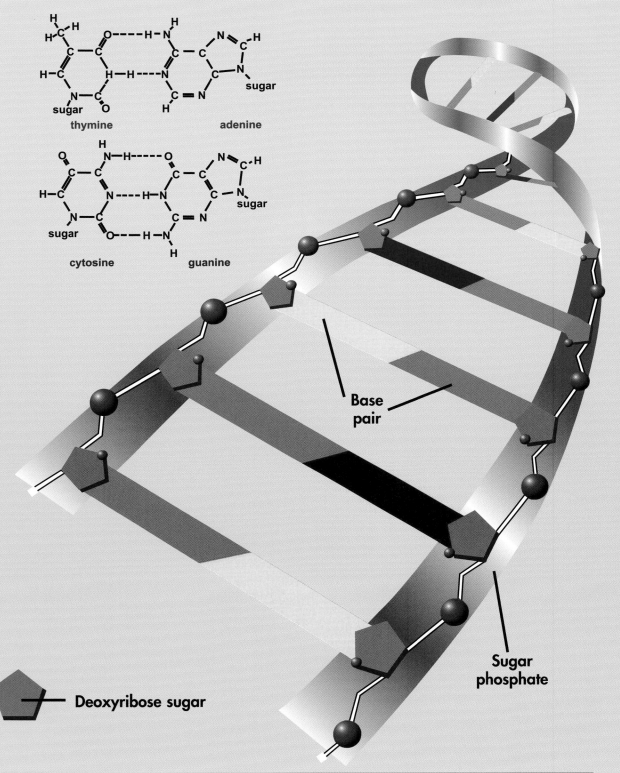

thymine   adenine

cytosine   guanine

Base pair

Sugar phosphate

Deoxyribose sugar

Nitrogen plays an important role in DNA. The main purpose of DNA is to store and transmit genetic information. This information will decide what color your hair and eyes will be, how tall you will grow, and much more. This information is held in the four nitrogen bases, thymine, adenine, cytosine, and guanine. The bases match up together to form base pairs *(upper-left corner)*. These base pairs are held together by a sugar phosphate backbone. This creates DNA's double helix structure, which supports a maze of complicated genetic information.

Enzymes such as nitrogenase are also made of protein. There are many enzymes in your body, and each of them serves a specific purpose. Each enzyme in your body speeds up a specific chemical reaction. For example, an enzyme called lysozyme, found in your tears, speeds up a reaction that destroys a certain bacteria. In this way, lysozyme in your tears protects your eyes from bacterial infection. Without enzymes, many reactions in the body would be too slow to support life.

It may sound like protein is just one substance, but it is actually made up of building blocks called amino acids. Scientists have found twenty different amino acids in protein. These amino acids are linked together in various combinations to form thousands of kinds of proteins. During digestion, the protein in food is broken back down into amino acids. Your body can then use these "blocks" to make new body proteins.

How does your body know how to arrange the amino acids into specific proteins? That is the work of another nitrogen-containing molecule called DNA. DNA contains a code that specifies the order in which the amino acids should be linked. These codes are used to make all of the different kinds of proteins found in your body. Each person has his or her own DNA, and no two people's DNA are exactly alike (except in identical twins). It is our DNA that makes us different from each other. You can thank nitrogen for that!

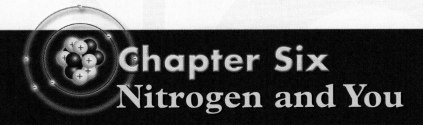

Most people have heard of the element nitrogen, but they do not really know how much it affects them. Nitrogen is involved in our lives in many ways. Sometimes, nitrogen can act in a destructive way, but many times it serves to make our lives easier, safer, and more exciting. Once people get to know nitrogen, they are able to see what an interesting element it really is.

Nitrogen Dioxide Pollution

Some of the worst air pollutants are nitrogen compounds. Whenever fossil fuels (such as oil, gas, or coal) are burned, nitrogen oxides are produced. Though power stations, schools, homes, and offices all produce nitrogen oxides, automobile exhaust accounts for more than half of the nitrogen oxides in polluted air. The heat from your car's hot engine forms nitrogen monoxide, just like lightning does. When this poisonous gas reacts with oxygen, it forms nitrogen dioxide. This foul-smelling brown gas is one of the main components of smog, the brown haze that is seen hanging over some urban areas. Nitrogen dioxide also dissolves in rainwater and forms nitric acid, one of the ingredients in acid rain. Acid rain kills fish and vegetation and eats away at buildings and statues. Nitrogen dioxide is a common outdoor pollutant, but it can also pollute the inside of your house! It comes from fireplaces, gas stoves, and water heaters. Nitrogen dioxide can irritate your eyes, nose, and throat. It can also make it easier for you to get lung infections. You can keep this gas from building up in your house by opening up windows and vents.

Nitrogen Saving Lives

Car air bags have saved many lives since they were first invented in 1968, but how do they work? An air bag's job is to provide a cushion between

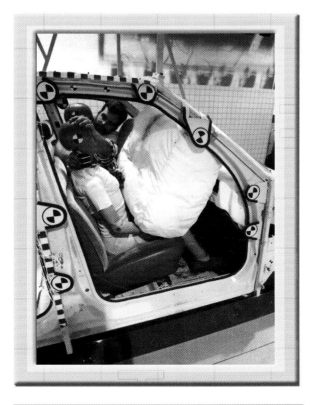

Nitrogen gas can also be a lifesaver. Its ability to expand rapidly plays a key role in air bags in cars.

the passengers and the car. It does this with the help of nitrogen gas. Wherever an air bag is located in the car, it is accompanied by a sensor. During a collision, the sensor sets off an explosive reaction that instantly produces hot blasts of nitrogen gas. As you know, gases expand. It is the rapid expansion of the nitrogen gas within the air bag that causes the bag to inflate in a split second, thus saving lives.

Finding a Criminal

Whenever you touch something, you leave behind evidence, with finger-prints. We are all born with unique ridges on our fingertips. Look closely at your fingers. The patterns you see are unlike those on anyone

Here, a police officer dusts for fingerprints at a crime lab. The dust contains silver nitrate ($AgNO_3$). This substance highlights the oils from a person's fingerprints. Once the fingerprints are found, they can be matched to others to help identify suspects or locate missing persons.

else's fingertips in the world. Since your fingertips are coated with a film of oily perspiration, your fingerprint is left behind on the surface of the things you touch.

Investigators can use fingerprints to identify people who are suffering with amnesia (memory loss), victims of accidents, and, of course, suspects of crimes. However, fingerprints are often invisible. That is why compounds like silver nitrate ($AgNO_3$) are important. Silver nitrate can be sprayed on surfaces, such as paper. Exposure to light causes a reaction that turns the print a brownish color. The print can then be photographed and used for identification.

Liquid Nitrogen and the Entertainment Business

If you have ever been to Disney World, you have probably seen liquid nitrogen in action. Liquid nitrogen is used at theme parks, in stage plays, and in movies to create the illusion of fog or mist. At room temperature, 77°F (25°C), liquid nitrogen has the appearance of boiling water. That is because it is already boiling. Remember: liquid nitrogen boils at a temperature of -320.44°F (-195.8°C), a temperature much colder than room temperature. This "cold fog" is perfect for creating the creepy effect of a witch's brew or the billowy white puffs of a dragon's breath.

Nitrogen is all around you. The air that surrounds you is literally filled with it. Although it took a while for scientists to notice this element, you have seen that nitrogen does a lot of important and interesting things. Fertilizer made with nitrogen supplies us with food, while the chill of liquid nitrogen makes sure food reaches our table fresh. Nitrogen can help us identify people, and it can provide us with entertainment. It is found in your muscles and organs, and it keeps the reactions in your body running smoothly. Nitrogen affects us in so many ways. It is amazing how much one little element can do!

The Periodic Table of Elements

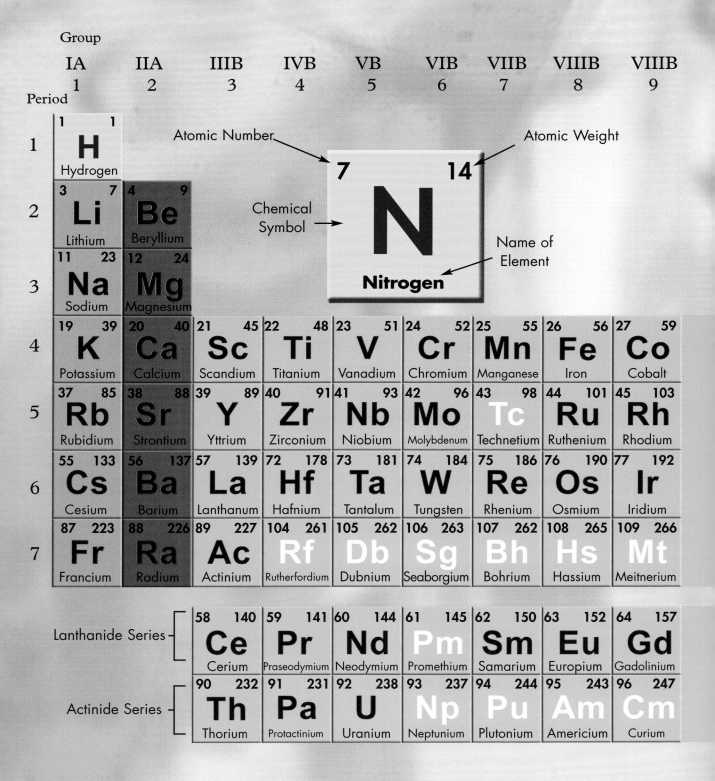

Group	IA	IIA	IIIB	IVB	VB	VIB	VIIB	VIIIB	VIIIB
Period	1	2	3	4	5	6	7	8	9

Atomic Number → 7

Atomic Weight → 14

Chemical Symbol → N

Name of Element → Nitrogen

	1 H Hydrogen (1)								
1									
2	3 Li 7 Lithium	4 Be 9 Beryllium							
3	11 Na 23 Sodium	12 Mg 24 Magnesium							
4	19 K 39 Potassium	20 Ca 40 Calcium	21 Sc 45 Scandium	22 Ti 48 Titanium	23 V 51 Vanadium	24 Cr 52 Chromium	25 Mn 55 Manganese	26 Fe 56 Iron	27 Co 59 Cobalt
5	37 Rb 85 Rubidium	38 Sr 88 Strontium	39 Y 89 Yttrium	40 Zr 91 Zirconium	41 Nb 93 Niobium	42 Mo 96 Molybdenum	43 Tc 98 Technetium	44 Ru 101 Ruthenium	45 Rh 103 Rhodium
6	55 Cs 133 Cesium	56 Ba 137 Barium	57 La 139 Lanthanum	72 Hf 178 Hafnium	73 Ta 181 Tantalum	74 W 184 Tungsten	75 Re 186 Rhenium	76 Os 190 Osmium	77 Ir 192 Iridium
7	87 Fr 223 Francium	88 Ra 226 Radium	89 Ac 227 Actinium	104 Rf 261 Rutherfordium	105 Db 262 Dubnium	106 Sg 263 Seaborgium	107 Bh 262 Bohrium	108 Hs 265 Hassium	109 Mt 266 Meitnerium

Lanthanide Series	58 Ce 140 Cerium	59 Pr 141 Praseodymium	60 Nd 144 Neodymium	61 Pm 145 Promethium	62 Sm 150 Samarium	63 Eu 152 Europium	64 Gd 157 Gadolinium
Actinide Series	90 Th 232 Thorium	91 Pa 231 Protactinium	92 U 238 Uranium	93 Np 237 Neptunium	94 Pu 244 Plutonium	95 Am 243 Americium	96 Cm 247 Curium

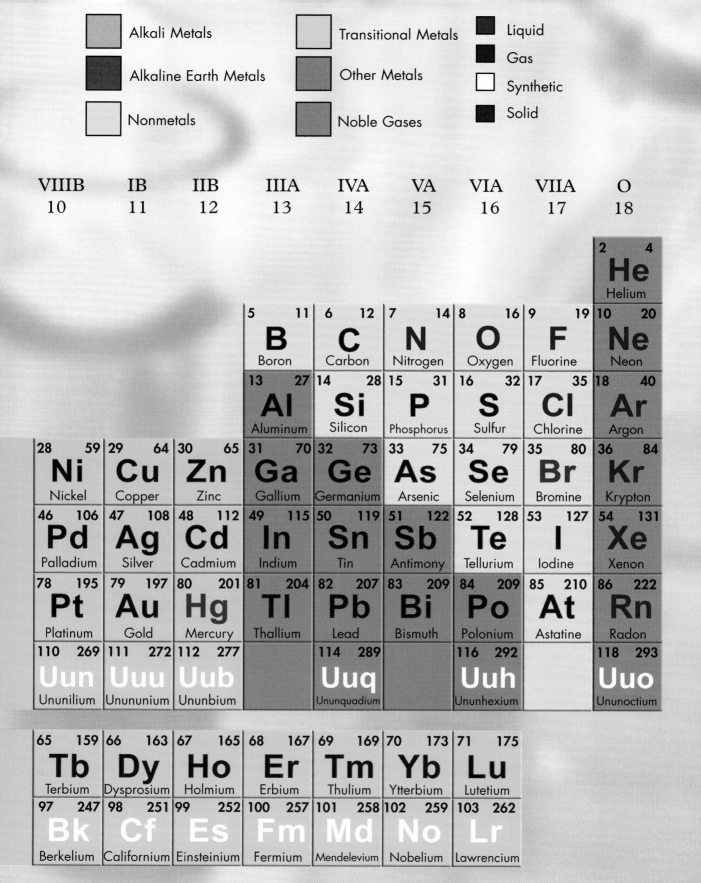

# Glossary

atmosphere The air that surrounds Earth.

atom The smallest part of an element having the chemical properties of that element.

bacteria Single-celled organisms that break down wastes and bodies of dead organisms, the products of which will then be reused by other animals.

bond An attractive force that links two atoms together.

chemical reaction A change in which one kind of matter is turned into another kind of matter.

denitrification The reduction of nitrates by bacteria; usually results in the escape of nitrogen into the air.

energy The ability to do work (or produce heat).

genetic Dealing with the variation and makeup of organisms.

mass The amount of matter in something.

matter What things are made of, something that takes up space and has mass.

molecule A group of atoms that are chemically bonded together.

photosynthesis The process in which green plants make their own food from sunlight, water, and a gas called carbon dioxide.

soluble Able to be dissolved in liquid.

symbol Something, such as a letter, abbreviation, or image, that stands for something else.

urban Of or relating to the city.

volume The amount of space that something occupies.

Canada Science and Technology Museum
1867 St. Laurent Boulevard
Ottawa, Ontario K1G 5A3
Canada
(613) 991-3044
Web site: http://www.sciencetech.technomuses.ca/english/index.cfm

Milton J. Rubenstein Museum of Science & Technology
500 South Franklin Street
Syracuse, NY 13202
(315) 425-9068
Web site: http://www.most.org

Montshire Museum of Science
One Montshire Road
Norwich, VT 05055
(802) 649-2200
Web site: http://www.montshire.net

Web Sites

Due to the changing nature of Internet links, the Rosen Publishing Group, Inc., has developed an online list of Web sites related to the subject of this book. This site is updated regularly. Please use this link to access the list:

http://www.rosenlinks.com/uept/nitr

For Further Reading

Gardner, Robert. *Kitchen Chemistry: Science Experiments to Do at Home*. New York: Julian Messner, 1988.

Greenwood, N. N., and A. Earnshaw. *Chemistry of the Elements*. St. Louis, MO: Elsevier, 1997.

Hudson, John. *The History of Chemistry*. New York: Kluwer Academic Publishers, 1992.

Newton, David E. *The Chemical Elements*. New York: Franklin Watts, 1994.

Stwertka, Albert. *A Guide to the Elements*. 2nd ed. New York: Oxford University Press, 1999.

Yount, Lisa. *Antoine Lavoisier: Founder of Modern Chemistry* (Great Minds of Science). Springfield, NJ: Enslow Publishers, 1997.

Bibliography

Brady, James E., and John R. Holum. *Chemistry: The Study of Matter and Its Changes*. New York: John Wiley & Sons, Inc., 1993.

Ebbing, Darrell D. *General Chemistry*. 4th ed. Boston: Houghton Mifflin Company, 1996.

Heiserman, David L. *Exploring Chemical Elements and Their Compounds*. New York: McGraw-Hill, 1991.

Stwertka, Albert. *A Guide to the Elements*. 2nd ed. New York: Oxford University Press, 1999.

Weeks, Mary Elvira. *Discovery of the Elements*. Ann Arbor, MI: UMI, 1968.

Index

About the Author

Heather Elizabeth Hasan graduated college summa cum laude with a dual major in biochemistry and chemistry. She currently resides in Montgomery County, Maryland, with her husband, Omar, and her son, Samuel.

Photo Credits

Cover, pp. 1, 9, 12, 14, 16, 17, 20, 22, 31, 33, 36, 42–43 by Tahara Hasan; p. 5 © Bettmann/Corbis; p. 7 (top left) courtesy of NASA; pp. 7 (top right), 39 © AP/Wide World Photos; p. 7 (bottom left) © 2002–2004 Custom Medical Stock Photo; p. 24 © David Taylor/Photo Researchers, Inc.; p. 25 © Larry Kolvoord/The Image Works; p. 26 © Antonia Reeve/Photo Researchers, Inc.; p. 29 © Corbis; pp. 30, 34 by Maura McConnell; p. 40 © Syracuse Newspapers/Carl J. Single/The Image Works.

Special thanks to Rosemarie Alken and Westtown School, in Westtown, Pennsylvania.

Designer: Tahara Hasan; Editor: Charles Hofer